LIFE STORY

FROG

MICHAEL CHINERY

Photography by
Barrie Watts

Illustrated by
Martin Camm

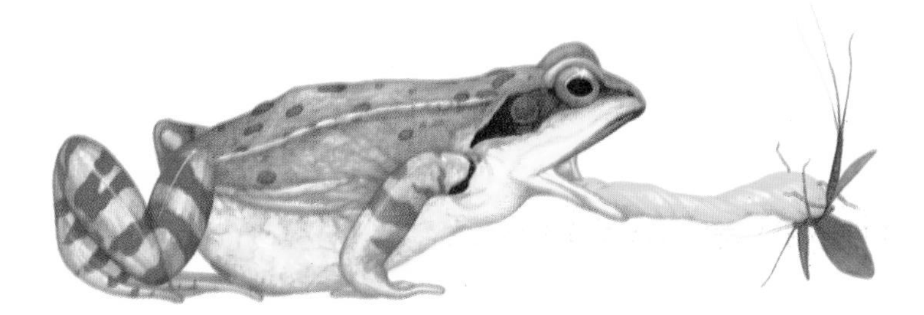

Troll Associates

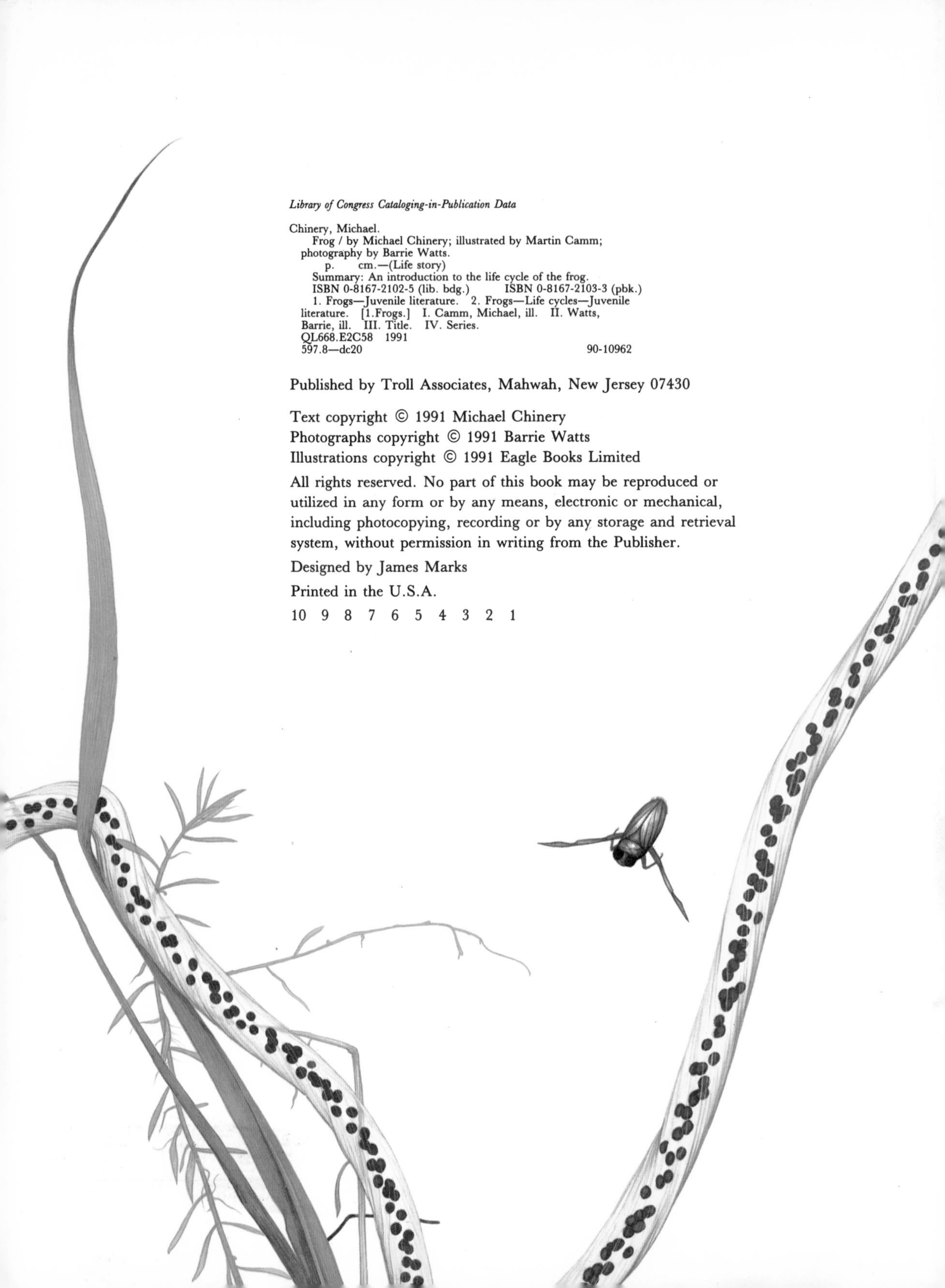

Library of Congress Cataloging-in-Publication Data

Chinery, Michael.
Frog / by Michael Chinery; illustrated by Martin Camm;
photography by Barrie Watts.
p. cm.—(Life story)
Summary: An introduction to the life cycle of the frog.
ISBN 0-8167-2102-5 (lib. bdg.) ISBN 0-8167-2103-3 (pbk.)
1. Frogs—Juvenile literature. 2. Frogs—Life cycles—Juvenile
literature. [1.Frogs.] I. Camm, Michael, ill. II. Watts,
Barrie, ill. III. Title. IV. Series.
QL668.E2C58 1991
597.8—dc20 90-10962

Published by Troll Associates, Mahwah, New Jersey 07430

Designed by James Marks

Printed in the U.S.A.

10 9 8 7 6 5 4 3 2 1

INTRODUCTION

A frog is equally at home on land and in the water. It spends the first few weeks of its life as a legless, fishlike tadpole which looks nothing like a frog. But then it begins to change. This book will show you how the tadpole grows legs and loses its tail, and how it changes its shape to become a little frog. You will also meet some of the many enemies that catch and eat frogs at all stages of their lives.

This bright-eyed animal is a common frog. It belongs to a group called amphibians, which means that it spends part of its life on land and part in the water. It never goes far from ponds or streams at any time.

Look at the frog's big back legs. They help it to jump around on the land and to swim strongly in the water.

The toad is a cousin of the frog, but its skin is more bumpy instead of smooth.

Frogs sleep all through the winter. Male frogs often sleep in the mud at the bottom of the pond. Female frogs prefer to sleep on land. They may hide under stones or in the garden.

The males wake up first in the spring. You may see them in the ponds with just their heads poking out of the water. They croak by day and night, and if there are many males together, they sound like motorcycles roaring in the distance. They must watch out for herons, who like to eat frogs.

Female frogs are much fatter than males because they are full of eggs. When a female reaches the pond after her winter sleep, a male will help her lay her eggs. The male does this by holding on to her tightly and squeezing her. The female can squirt up to 3,000 black, jelly-covered eggs into the water. The male then fertilizes the eggs in the water. Usually, this is all done at night, the safest time. The fertilized eggs are left behind. The male and female frogs have not eaten during the winter months, and they are weak and hungry. Some females are so weak, in fact, that they die after laying their eggs.

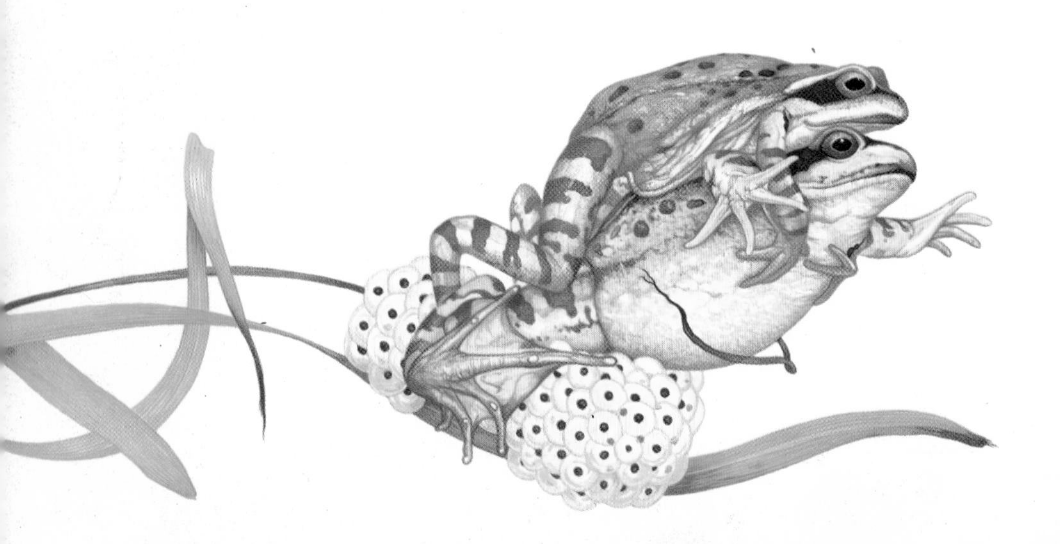

Each little egg is surrounded by a layer of jelly. This jelly swells up when it gets into the water to produce the slippery mass called frog spawn. The jelly helps to protect the eggs from most of their enemies. It is too slippery for many animals to grab hold of. The little ball of eggs laid by one female can swell to the size of a football.

The photograph shows two big blobs of spawn. The darker one has just been laid. You can find frog spawn in the ponds in February in warm areas, but where it is colder you won't find it until April or even May. You can tell toad spawn from frog spawn, because toad spawn forms long strings instead of shapeless blobs.

The frog's eggs are perfectly round when they are laid. They become oval after a few days. Then they become commalike as they turn into little tadpoles. The spawn in the photograph is about ten days old and you can see the tadpoles inside the jelly.

The tadpoles have been living on food stored in the egg, but soon they must leave the jelly to look for food. The exact time needed for the eggs to turn into tadpoles depends on the weather. Everything speeds up when it is warm, so the warmer the weather, the quicker the tadpoles will hatch.

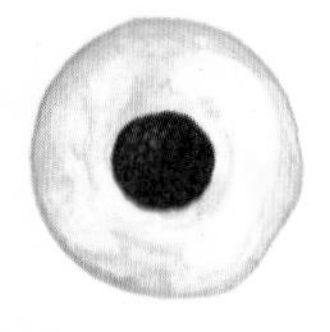

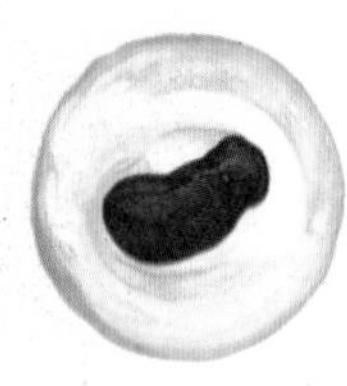

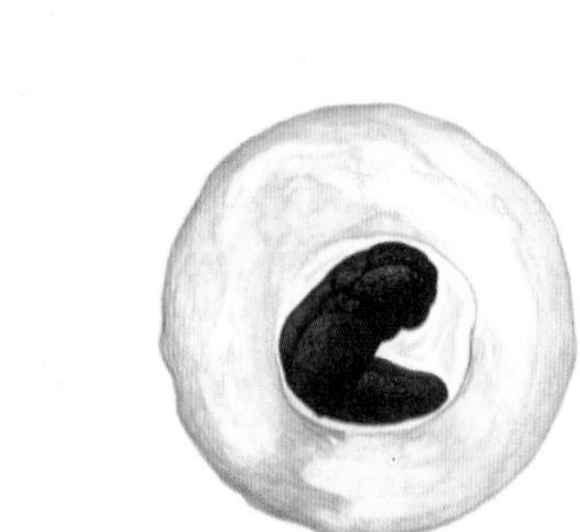

Two weeks after the frog spawn was laid these tadpoles pushed their way out of the jelly. They cover the jelly with their wriggling black bodies. Each tadpole clings to the jelly with a little sucker under its head. You can see the sucker in the drawing.

Look at the feathery growths behind the tadpole's head. These are gills and they help the tadpole to breathe. The gills take oxygen from the water and pass it to the tadpole's bloodstream.

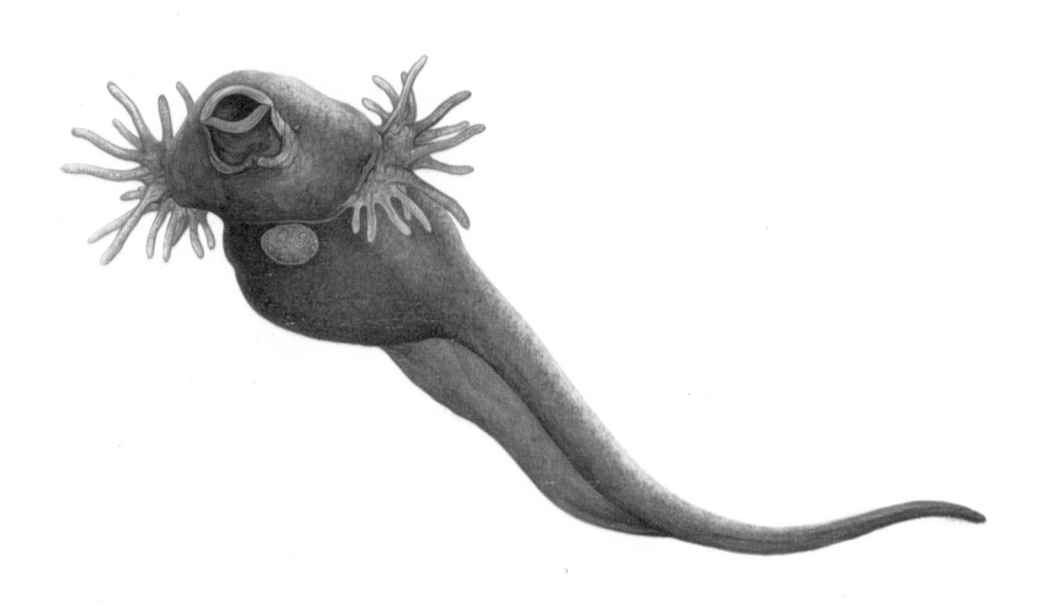

Now the tadpoles want to eat. Their main food is the green scum that seems to cover everything in the pond. This scum is made up of tiny green plants called algae.

The tadpoles grow quickly. The one in the photograph is about two weeks old. It has lost its feathery gills and it looks like a little fish. Inside its body it has new gills.

Water goes in through the tadpole's mouth and is pumped over the gills. The water then escapes through the spiracle, which is a small hole on the left side of the tadpole's body.

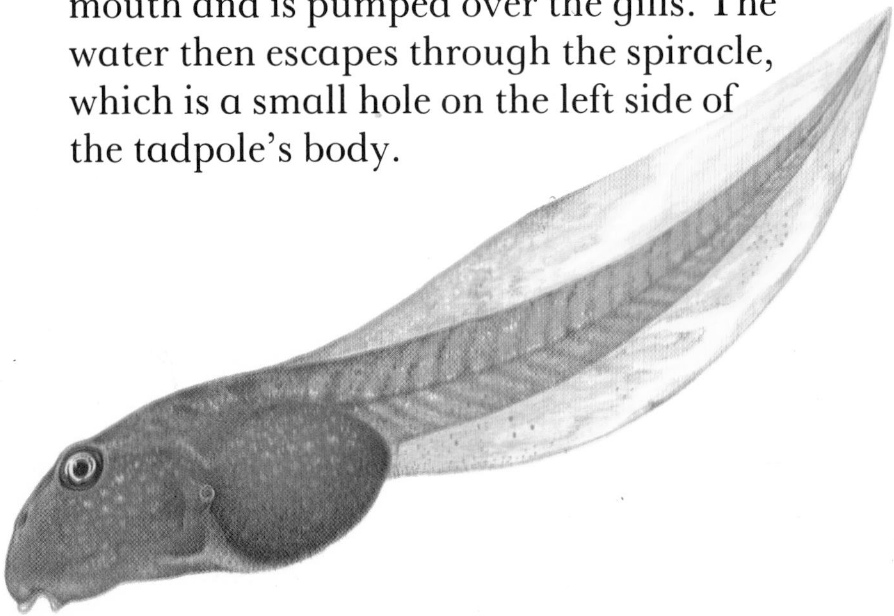

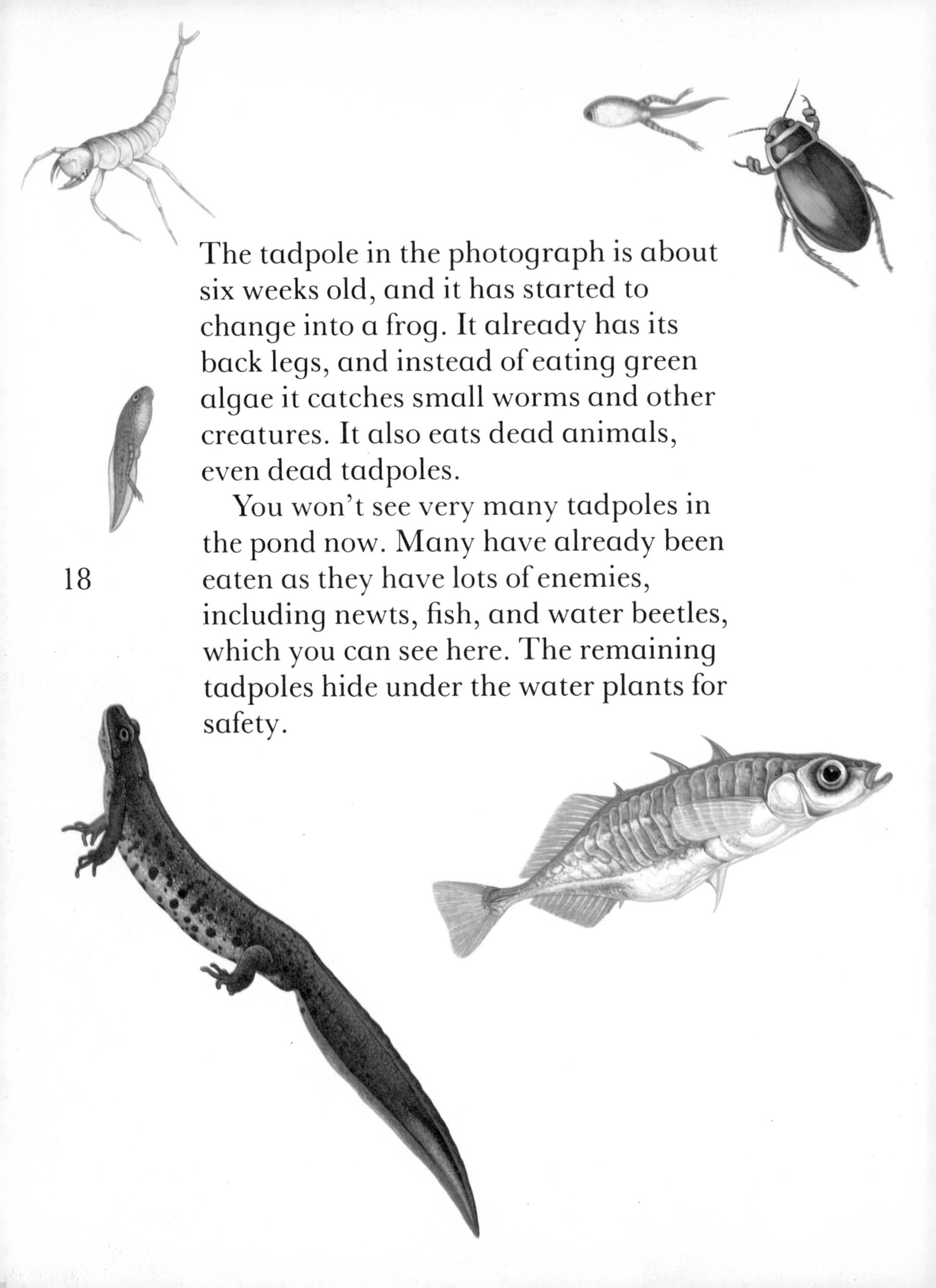

The tadpole in the photograph is about six weeks old, and it has started to change into a frog. It already has its back legs, and instead of eating green algae it catches small worms and other creatures. It also eats dead animals, even dead tadpoles.

You won't see very many tadpoles in the pond now. Many have already been eaten as they have lots of enemies, including newts, fish, and water beetles, which you can see here. The remaining tadpoles hide under the water plants for safety.

The tadpole is now ten weeks old and is really beginning to look like a little frog. Its left front leg is growing out through the spiracle. The right leg will soon break through on the other side of the body. The tadpole can't use its gills for breathing anymore, because the spiracle is blocked.

The tadpole now has small lungs, rather like ours, and it comes to the surface to gulp air into them from time to time. It can also get oxygen from the water through its skin.

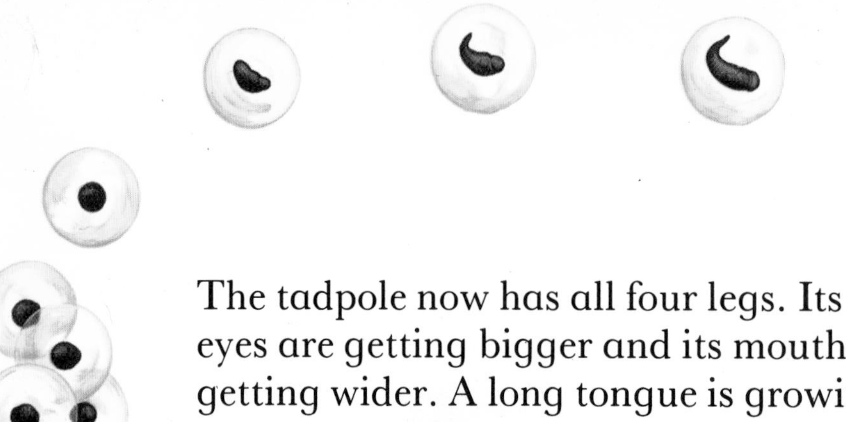

The tadpole now has all four legs. Its eyes are getting bigger and its mouth is getting wider. A long tongue is growing inside its mouth. The tadpole can't eat anything at this stage, but it won't starve. Its tail slowly shrinks back into its body and this gives the frog the food it needs.

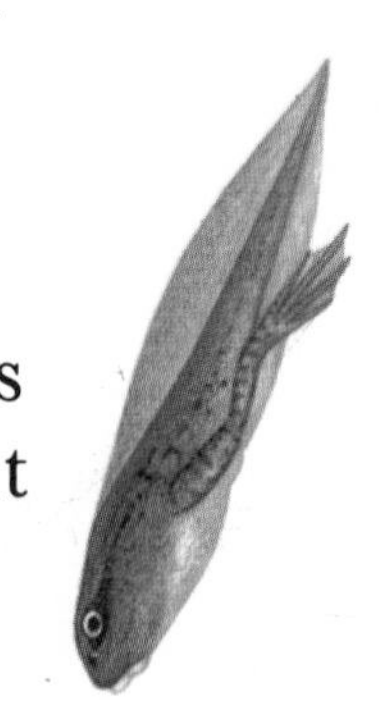

The tadpole doesn't need a tail now because it can swim with its long back legs. The change from tadpole to frog is almost complete now. It has been about twelve weeks since the tadpole left its jelly.

With its tail almost gone, the tadpole is now a young frog. It struggles out of the water and often sits on floating leaves. It is ready to move to the land, but it must stay in damp places and watch out for new enemies.

Many birds, snakes, and other animals like eating young frogs. Most of the frog's time will be spent eating, but when fall comes, it will look for a safe place to sleep through the winter.

The young frog spends two or three years on land before it is fully grown and ready to go back to the pond to mate. During this time it eats worms, flies, slugs, snails, and many other small creatures.

To catch the animals, the frog flicks out its sticky tongue and brings them back to its mouth. The whole action is over in a split second. The food is swallowed whole. The frog always blinks when it swallows, because it uses its eyeballs to push the food down its throat.

The frog uses its strong back legs to hop everywhere. Most hops are quite short, but the frog is also a good long jumper. If it is frightened, a frog can leap nearly two feet. It often leaps into the pond to escape from its enemies. This won't always save a frog from its main enemy, the snake. The snake will follow it into the water.

Frogs that are not eaten can live for more than ten years, but few ever reach this age. Of the 3,000 eggs in the original frog spawn, only about 100 will become young frogs. Out of these young frogs only about five will grow into adult frogs. But those who survive will help create a new generation.

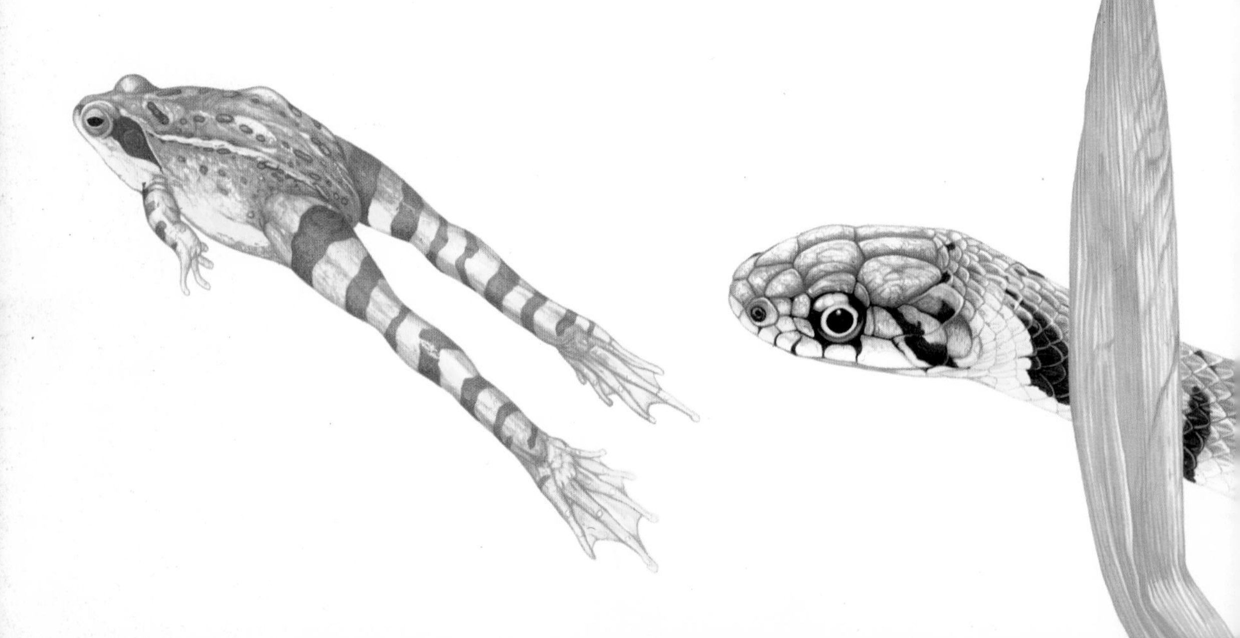

Fascinating facts

The world's largest frog is the Goliath frog, which lives in West Africa. Its body may be more than one foot long and it can weigh more than six pounds.

The world's smallest frog lives in Cuba and its body is sometimes no more than half an inch long. It has no English name.

Some frogs living in South America are called dart-poison frogs. Their skins are

Goliath frog

very poisonous and some Indian tribes use the poison on their hunting arrows. The animals that they shoot die very quickly.

Tree frogs have little suction pads on their toes. They spend a lot of time in trees and the pads help them to cling to leaves. The frogs can even cling to window-panes. Some tree frogs never come down to the ground. Their tadpoles grow up in little ponds that form in the forks of branches.

The male mouth-brooding frog appears to eat the eggs after they have been laid, but he actually keeps them safe in a pouch in his throat. The tadpole stage is completed inside the eggs, and when the eggs hatch, the father spits out tiny frogs.

American tree frog

Index